# Frank Lloyd Wright
## AT A GLANCE

# USONIAN
# HOUSES

# Frank Lloyd Wright
## AT A GLANCE

# USONIAN HOUSES

### Doreen Ehrlich

PRC

First published 2002 by

PRC Publishing Ltd,

64 Brewery Road, London N7 9NT

A member of **Chrysalis** Books plc


Distributed in the U.S. and Canada by:

Sterling Publishing Co., Inc.

387 Park Avenue South

New York, NY 10016

ISBN 1 85648 645 1


Printed and bound in China

FRONTISPIECE: Exterior of living room with fretwork screen on the
left from the Pope Leighey House.

ACKNOWLEDGMENTS

The publisher wishes to thank those who kindly supplied the photography for this
    book. All photography was taken by Simon Clay, with the exception of the
    following:

Pages 3 (detail), 12, 73, 74-75, 77 (both) and 96 (detail), courtesy of © Robert
    P. Ruschak;
Pages 39, 79, 81, 83, 90 and 91, courtesy of Alan Weintraub/Arcaid;
A. C. Lellis Andrade kindly supplied the photograph on page 41 (top);
Page 85 courtesy of Allen Memorial Art Museum (photographer: David Calco).
Cover photography:
Simon Clay for front cover and back cover (middle and bottom).
© Bettmann/CORBIS for back cover (top).

# CONTENTS

# INTRODUCTION

In 1929 the stock market crash and the Great Depression that followed put a virtual end to building activity in the United States. The years of national reevaluation and reform that followed provided a strong impetus for a radical change of direction for architects and planners, not just in the realm of public building but also in domestic architecture. There was a real and urgent need for low-cost housing for large numbers of people that would be appropriate for a modern, democratic society. Frank Lloyd Wright responded to this need by applying his lifelong principles of organic architecture to what he was to term the Usonian house. The radical designs, which were for middle-income families, contributed greatly to the triumphant rescue of his reputation among the general public which had been severely affected by the publicity surrounding the scandals and tragedy of his personal life in the early decades of the century.

Wright's capacity for reinventing himself and responding to changing social and economic climates is a marked and constant feature of his long and productive career. The last quarter century of Wright's extraordinarily creative life included such landmarks as the setting up of the Taliesin Fellowship and Taliesin West, which ensured the training and productivity of the next generation of Wright-trained architects, the building of the Guggenheim Museum, New York, and the Marin County Administration complex, California. In the domestic domain his major achievements were Fallingwater and the Usonian house, both regarded as mold-breaking concepts in their time and as key contributions to the history of Western architecture in the 20th century ever since. In the 40s and 50s, the Usonian designs brought Wright popularity because they were

RIGHT: POPE LEIGHEY HOUSE. Living area. The open-plan living area with flexible seating and views to the garden was a key component of the Usonian house as was the use of economical natural materials, brick, wood, concrete, and glass. Windows are integrated into the design and distinctive cut-out panels are used for clerestory windows and light screens.

LEFT: POPE LEIGHEY HOUSE. Study area. Built-in furniture and sufficient storage space was an essential component of the compact spaces. Specially designed modular seating can be moved into flexible arrangements for different activities. The cool blue of the upholstery and carpet complements the prevailing earth-red tones of the paneling and brick.

seen to address the real needs of middle-income families in times of unprecedented economic uncertainty. The fact that Wright was able to realize the house so speedily within a strict budget and without the seemingly idiosyncratic and exotic qualities that had distinguished his domestic work for previous, wealthier clients, further ensured their success.

By January 1938, a portrait of Wright featured as the front cover of *Time*, with the heading "Frank Lloyd Wright, Usonian Architect," and a long illustrated article detailing recent projects, including the Johnson Wax Building, Fallingwater, and the Jacobs House by an architect thought by many to be a spent force at 63. Wright was later to use the term Usonian broadly to include some 140 houses built to his design between 1936 and 1959, the year of his death. These houses shared certain key characteristics, most notably in their layout and system of construction, although as the idea developed over the near-quarter century of their building there was a great variety in their form, budgets, and materials of construction. Their influence on later 20th- century domestic design in the United States and elsewhere is wide reaching. The ideas realized in these modest homes helped change the reality of small house construction and have been subsumed into the design of living spaces ever since.

Wright appears to have used the eye-catching term "Usonia" to set his work apart from others as early as 1927, while his full Usonian manifesto was published in the prestigious *Architectural Forum* in 1938, which devoted an issue almost entirely to some 30 recent projects by Wright including Fallingwater and the Jacobs House. The meaning of "Usonia" became adaptable to different uses, and the origins of the term are somewhat opaque. In *An Autobiography*, first published in 1932, Wright uses the term to refer to the houses, but soon it becomes part of the larger context of his ideal, decentralized, democratic community in which the houses were to be built. "Usonia" then refers to the utopian integrated society of the architect's dream of the future.

Wright's experiments with the radical reworking of the private space of the family had begun while he was in his 20s with his own family home and studio practice in Oak Park, Illinois, in the 1890s. These years also saw publication of his designs for "A Small House with Lots of Room in It" as well as his building of grand houses for affluent clients. The houses that made his name and established his international reputation in the latter years of the 19th century and the early years of the 20th, the Prairie houses, were distinguished by their custom-made designs. Throughout the quintessential Prairie house, the Robie House (1908–1910) in Chicago for example, the design elements are integrated to an unprecedented degree, including Wright-designed built-in furniture and lighting fixtures, and textiles which used the same motifs as the window glass. Each Usonian

ABOVE: POPE LEIGHEY HOUSE. Exterior view. A key feature of the early Usonian houses was the use of less expensive natural materials such as timber and brick which could be standardized from house to house. The timber was left in a relatively natural state so that the nature of the material could be seen.

LEFT: BAZETT HOUSE. Living room with dining area and hearth. A grid of hexagons (the module on which the house is built) is incised into the concrete floor pad which is the source of the integral gravity heating throughout the house. The dining area is served by the workspace (which is lit by a skylight) behind the hearth.

house was adapted to the wishes of its owner, who was asked to supply a "wants list," whether it was for storage for home-preserved produce in cupboards that were accessible to an owner who was five foot two, a living room that could be used as a space for performing chamber music, or sufficient bedrooms for a large family of children.

The Prairie house era which ensured Wright an international reputation, had come to an end nearly a generation before the invention of the Usonian house. Wright decided in 1909 that "...I was losing my grip on work and even interest in it." Abandoning his wife and family in Oak Park, he decamped to Europe with the wife of a client and the personal tragedy that then ensued meant that his reputation among the general public was dogged by scandalous media reportage for many years to come. During the 1920s, Wright was building concrete textile block houses for wealthy clients in California while completing work on his major public building of the period, the Imperial Hotel, Tokyo—an extraordinarily complex construction (now demolished) which withstood one of the worst earthquakes in the history of Japan and helped reestablish his professional reputation. From this period, Wright entered a remarkable final phase of creativity, which brought him and his work back into the architectural limelight and to the center of public attention, further fostered by his lecture tours, television appearances, and many publications.

Wright explained that he had adopted the term "Usonia," which appears in his writings in the late 20s, from the Victorian novelist Samuel Butler who had used it to describe a mythologized United States in his Utopian novel *Erewhon* ("Nowhere" spelled backward). By May 1939, when Wright gave a series of lectures at the Royal Institute of British Architects, he was using "Usonia" to differentiate North Americans from others, "Because we have not a monopoly of that title...and "United Statesers" doesn't sound well...Your Samuel Butler

RIGHT: ROSENBAUM HOUSE. Exterior with carport. Horizontal lines and ground-hugging contours and roofs with broad, protective overhangs are key features of the Usonian house. The use of carports, rather than enclosed garages reinforces the horizontality of the designs and enhances their seemingly natural integration into the site.

called us 'Usonians.' I think Usonian an excellent name, having its roots in union, as we have our national life in it. So I use the term and hope to get the country used to it in good time."

Wright went on to explain his practical application of the idea to "a newer Usonia, expressing the inner spirit of our democracy, which by and large is not yet so very democratic after all, as you may know." In his lectures Wright used slides of the Hanna House and the Jacobs House along with Fallingwater and the S.C. Johnson Administration Building and the Johnson residence, Wingspread, as examples of his most recent work. Both the Hanna and Jacobs House were quintessential Usonian houses, part of a series of small houses that realized distinctive architectural design and the individuality of the owner but at an economical price in sharp distinction to the luxurious Fallingwater and Wingspread.

Wright's London lecture series, which reached a wider audience with publication, was entitled "An Organic Architecture: the Architecture of Democracy," and delivered as it was just before World War II began, the series had a particular resonance and did much to enhance Wright's international reputation.

The first Usonian to be built, the Jacobs House, demonstrates several key Wrightian concepts which it shares with the earlier Prairie houses and Fallingwater. The most significant of these is its integration with its site. Fallingwater, famously, is cantilevered over a waterfall on a spectacular site at Mill Run, Pennsylvania, and Wright's aim of working with nature is similarly apparent in the modest Jacobs House. Wright's radical desire throughout his long working life to "break the box" of conventional architecture and to make indoors and out as unified as possible, connecting the "vista within" to "the vista without" put him into opposition with the international style of his modernist contemporaries, such as Mies van de Rohe and Le

Corbusier. Le Corbusier, in particular, considered a house to be "a machine for living in" regardless of site, nationality, or cultural differences.

However, Wright is nearer in practice to this younger generation of architects in the interior design of the Usonian house, although he would never have admitted any affinity to those he termed "The Bauhaus Boys." He believed that in the interests of regarding the whole interior space as an integral unit, doors, windows, and other openings should be conceived as part of an integrated structure, and that all necessary fittings, and indeed as much furniture as was practicable, should be built-in, to give his much-prized qualities of "simplicity and repose."

As several Usonian homes were, in the interests of economy, part worked upon by their owners, the fixtures and fittings offered opportunities for creative construction, although Wright's attention to detail remained acute and much of the furniture was built-in. The fact that the disposition of the interior space and the fixtures within it were determined allowed very little flexibility in the accumulation of objects. The owners of the Goetsch-Winckler House recalled removing a Bauhaus-designed chair when Wright was due to visit and replacing it when he had gone as they feared the architect's scorn at the intrusion of such an artefact of international modernism into one of his houses.

The first completed Usonian house was the Herbert and Katherine Jacobs House, completed in 1937. The house cost $5,500, which included the architect's fee, combining, as did many of the early Usonians "the magic of Wright's name" with "a price tag that made it all seem possible," as Herbert Jacobs wrote in his account of the house after it was completed. In contrast the Robie House of 1909 had cost

$35,000. Wright's aim in a changed society nearly 30 years later was to provide "modest-cost houses...there is nothing more interesting or more important in this world today than trying to put into the houses in which our typical best citizens live something of the quality of a genuine work of art."

Wright devised a technologically radical construction and assembly process for the early Usonians which satisfied both economic and aesthetic considerations. A concrete platform with heating pipes cast in it was sited on a drained gravel or crushed stone bed and formed the foundation of the house. Wright's favored concrete, his "gutter-rat" of building materials, which he used for such key structures as the Californian textile block houses and the Solomon Guggenheim Museum, New York, was, in the standard Usonian process mixed with red (Wright's favorite color) to provide a warm, earthy coloration throughout the house. Gravity heating provided a constant temperature without the need for radiators. On the base was erected the brick core of the house, around the kitchen area, or workspace as Wright was to term it, and its essential flues. In Wright's drawings and in the houses themselves, a unit module and geometrical grid were used, which made it possible for the early Usonians to be built by local contractors, or in some cases by the owners themselves, using standard materials in standard sizes, working

ABOVE: CARL SCHULTZ HOUSE. Saint Joseph, Michigan. Workspace. The Schultz House is built on a grand scale with expensive materials but retains essential components such as the workspace sited in the pivotal position of the living area at the back of the chimney. Clients were invited to state their storage and other needs and the height at which they wished cupboards and shelves to be put.

ABOVE: LOWELL WALTER HOUSE. Bedroom. The interiors of Usonian houses are remarkable for their simplicity and integral design and decoration. All superfluous free-standing furniture is eliminated and shelves and storage are constructed to the same module and often of the same materials as the house as a whole, thus achieving a remarkable unity of form.

to the module of the house, whether it be rectangular, hexagonal, or other geometric form, which was often inscribed in the concrete floor.

In his account of the building of the Jacobs House, Herbert Jacobs details the board-and-batten construction, ready-manufactured from pine (grained cypress was often used in later houses) which served as both exterior and interior finish, eliminating the necessity for interior wall coverings. The "ready made" walls were assembled at the site and were constructed of a sandwich of three layers of waterproofed plywood and two of heavy tarpaper, providing strength and good insu-

lation at an economic price. The roof was carried mainly by the masonry walls and was put up early in the construction process to provide shelter for the rest of the work. It consisted of three layers conventionally surfaced with asphalt felt, rising higher over the living and dining area and lower over the bedrooms and bathroom. These variations in height allowed the use of clerestory strips at the top of the walls, often cut in striking shapes, as both a decorative feature, providing a view of the tops of trees on the site, and a means of bringing light into the rooms where privacy was essential.

ABOVE: LOWELL WATER HOUSE. Garden Room. The Lowell Walter House is remarkable for its light-filled living area which uses skylights and clerestory windows in addition to floor-to-ceiling fenestration. More modest Usonians employed similar principles of indirect lighting, often through perforated wood screens with geometric patterns at ceiling height.

The patterned shadows cast through the clerestory windows were remembered long after as part of the unique atmosphere of the Usonian interior by those who had lived in them. Wright had used the device before in the pierced glazed patterns of the Californian concrete textile block houses of the 20s, while the floor-to-ceiling windows in the rooms requiring less privacy had formed part of his early designs for domestic interiors, providing the key component of a glass screen onto nature and bringing the outside inside.

This greater openness and increased fenestration may be seen as an updating and radical revision of the Prairie house, with which it shares its marked horizontality and close integration with the site. However, the Prairie house, though radical, was built for affluent clients with kitchen, living, and dining areas designed as separate spaces, however open in aspect. The Usonians responded to seismic changes in family life, especially to the changing status of women. As Wright himself explained, in the modern, servantless household, the woman of the house became the central figure, a "hostess 'officio' [instead of]...a kitchen mechanic behind closed doors." The kitchen itself was moved to the center of the house and renamed a "workspace." "Family processes are conveniently centralized" was his commentary in 1948 on Usonian principles, "so that the mistress of the house can turn a pancake with one hand while chucking the baby into a bath with the other."

With the kitchen workspace as the hub of the household, the new greater informality of domestic life could be accommodated. The formal dining room, which had once been regarded as a separate space, had lost its function and become an anachronism. Wright's solution to this problem, in the Jacobs House, for example, was to eliminate the dining room altogether, while a table made the connection between living and workspace areas. Externally a garage was deemed unnecessary and a carport was provided in its place.

Wright was always eager to share his ideas with the next generation and to encourage self-sufficiency and self-build with the clients' practical cooperation in fashioning the houses he designed. His lecture series at college campuses produced an enthusiastic response, "they one and all seem hungry for something...And that applies to buildings just as much or even more than anything else." Wright's dream of the future as a decentralized democratic community formed of clusters of Usonian houses in rural settings which he termed Broadacre City was first outlined in his *The Disappearing City* of 1932 and expounded in lectures, writings, and exhibitions but never built. The Usonian house, however evolved rapidly, to eventually include five variations adaptable to different clients' needs and contexts but all maintaining the original Usonian principles first seen in the Jacobs House. In 1953 a model Usonian house was built on the site of what is now the Solomon Guggenheim Museum in New York. The centerpiece of a major retrospective of Wright's work and recognized as crowning his career in his lifetime, it brought the reality of Usonian living to the widest possible public. Subsequent walk-through exhibitions of model Usonians only served to emphasize the continuing relevance and resonance of Wright's original idea.

# CASE STUDIES

# HANNA HOUSE

**Jean S. and Paul R. Hanna House "Honeycomb House"**
**Constructed:** 1936
**Address:** 737 Frenchman's Road, Stanford, California 94305.
Public tours by reservation only.

The Hanna House was particularly fortunate in its site as it was landscaped by Frederick Law Olmsted, the most illustrious landscape architect of his day as part of the nearby Palo Alto campus of Stanford University. The Hannas succeeded in finding a particularly spectacular location on the side of a hill in some 1.48 acres of land. Paul Hanna was a professor in Stanford's School of Education, and a new home was needed for a growing family of five. The Usonian houses were built in 17 states across the United States, and while all retain certain key characteristics, different modules were devised for the vastly different locations. None was more distinctive than the Hanna House, which is fashioned on the hexagon, a radical departure in Wright's work, giving the structure its popular name "the Honeycomb House." The use of the hexagon enabled greater flexibility in the design, allowing greater unity of exterior and interior spaces and conversion of the spaces to the changing needs of family life. The hexagon replaced the rectangle as Wright's favorite design module by reason of this very adaptablity.

The house is built of common wire-cut San Jose brick inside and out, and such was the flexibility offered by the choice of the hexagonal module and the typical wooden walls, that the spaces could be adapted to suit the family's changing lifestyle. The redwood boards which formed many of the walls could be disassembled and reassembled easily. Each redwood board and recessed batten was formed to be one foot,

RIGHT: View of the house from the terrace. Each floor continues the hexagonal motif, the garden terrace even has the hexagonal motif incised into its flooring blocks, a motif repeated in the concrete of the living room floor. The evocation of Japanese design that is so marked a feature of the house is echoed in the use of extensively glazed window walls onto the terraces and the splendid garden beyond. The windows have a linking rectangular design of simple mullions that form interesting and dramatic shadows in bright sunlight.

one inch, and so flexible were they that the walls of the workspace could open like louvers if required. The workspace and living room are all that remain of the original structure and Wright himself adapted most of the building around the brick chimney at its core. The adaptations and special nature of the design were expensive and whereas the original cost was estimated at $15,000, the final cost was $37,000 at a time of economic depression.

The building suffered major earthquake damage in 1989 and has since been restored at the cost of some $2 million taking ten years in a process of great complexity. The house was originally designed for a flat site and the complex placing of it on a hill in itself caused problems, exacerbated by the fact that it was discovered that the San Andreas fault lay under the hill. Wright was unconcerned by this when it was drawn to his attention. Famously, his vast Imperial Hotel had withstood the 1923 Tokyo earthquake because the foundations were

RIGHT: Exterior view showing the extensive range of windows and the marked horizontality of the design. The horizontal emphasis is reinforced by the bands of window mullions that exactly mirror the wooden board siding which is such a marked characteristic of the house, both externally and internally. The fine oak tree is an essential element of the picturesque setting.

so secure and several of the Californian textile block houses were built in areas of earthquake risk. Throughout his career Wright appeared to relish the challenge presented by problematic sites.

However even Wright's unshakeable confidence was no match 53 years later for Loma Prieta which caused unprecedented damage. The extraordinarily complex and expensive process of restoration revealed that the structure was essentially not reinforced, and although the house was reopened in 1999, great care is still needed in maintaining the accessibility of such an important national monument.

Despite the problems caused in its siting, it is possible to say that, to an even greater degree than many other Usonian houses, the Hanna House is fully integrated into its hilly site, as it appears to be wrapped round the hill. The organic unity of the building and its site is enhanced by the use of huge window walls onto the terrace and garden beyond. The windows have a linking rectangular design of simple muntins that form interesting shadow patterns in the interior in the bright Californian sunlight.

The hexagonal motif of the structure is continued in the smallest details of the design, being incised in the concrete floor both internally and externally, and forming the honeycomb shapes of many of the furnishings, designed by Wright, thus integrating the built-in furniture with such moveable elements as tables, chairs, and even cushions. The proliferation of honeycomb shapes extends even to the tiling of the bathroom.

The honeycomb motif employed at the Hanna House may be seen as a logical spatial bridging development in Wright's late flowering career to the circular shapes which dominate his final years, culminating in the design of the Solomon Guggenheim Museum, New York. Wright's lifelong passion for Japanese design was shared by Professor Hanna and his wife and this is realized in the lightness and elegance of the Honeycomb House.

ABOVE: View of the house from the courtyard. The hexagonal unit or honeycomb which gives the house its popular name is used consistently throughout its design both in its ground plan and elevation and in its interior and exterior detail. The floors, courtyard, and retaining walls are all built at an ascending gradient into the hillside which serves further to integrate the house into its spectacular setting. However, as it was built over the San Andreas fault, it received extensive damage in 1989 during the Loma Prieta earthquake which closed it to the public. The house has now been comprehensively restored and reopened.

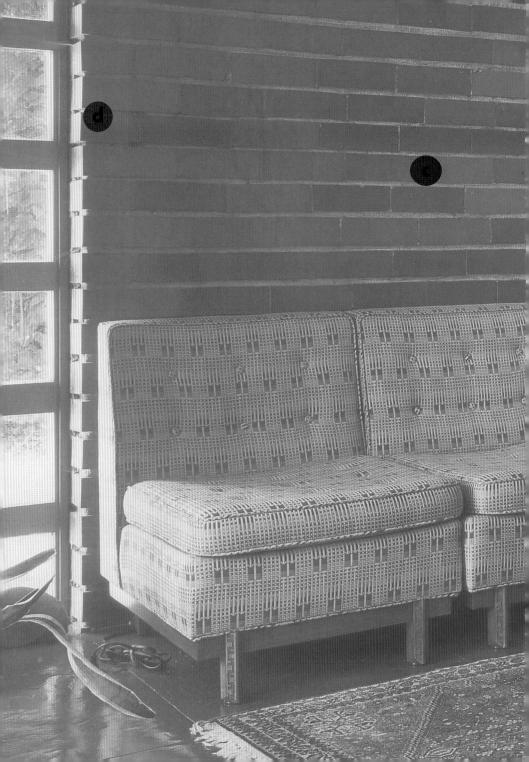

# JACOBS FIRST RESIDENCE

**Herbert and Katherine Jacobs First Residence**
**Constructed:** 1936
**Address:** 441 Toepfer Street, Madison (formerly Westmoreland),
Wisconsin.

The Jacobs House was the first built Usonian house and cost $5,500, which included the architect's fee. Wright himself closely supervised its construction from Taliesin, which was not far away. The Jacobs House was the first in which in Wright's words "the family processes are conveniently centralized," where the woman of the house was "no longer a mechanic behind closed doors," could cook in the newly designated "workspace," converse, and watch her children playing outside at one and the same time. This reflected Wright's response to huge changes in the pattern of family life although he assumed that the woman's place was still in the kitchen. Writing of a 1938 Usonian home in *Architectural Forum* in January 1948, he stated that while "the mistress of the house can turn a pancake with one hand while chucking the baby into a bath with the other," the man of the house is "meantime sitting at his dinner, lord of all."

A greater openness, both inside and out, is a key feature of the Jacobs House. Constructed around the garden or sun-court, with floor-to-ceiling windows, there is a marked visual and actual access to nature. Although the single-story house is only 1,340 square feet, much smaller than the typical Prairie house, it seems spacious. The Jacobs House is also more horizontal in emphasis than a Prairie house, rendering its position on the site more integrated and in Wright's terms organic.

RIGHT: Living room with windows opening to the terrace on the left. The technological innovations of the Usonian house were first used in the Jacobs House. These included the use of system-built construction which included the use of gravity heating in the concrete floor slab common to all the designs. In the Jacobs House the unit of construction, a two by four foot rectangle is incised into the floor slab which is stained red—a color complemented by the redwood paneling and warmth of the brick.

**a** Built-in components: a sense of space in a small area is created by streamlining essential amenities and, where possible, by building them into the design.

**b** Geometric forms used in an integrated design: the Jacobs House is built to a two by four foot rectangular module. The rectangular unit is scored into the concrete floor pad and the motif is repeated in the forms of the paneling and windows.

**c** Use of natural materials: brick, wood paneling, concrete, and glass predominate in Usonian design. As identical materials are used for the exterior and interior, the outside is brought inside, creating an organic whole.

**d** Light filled spaces: natural light is brought into the street side of the house by the use of clerestory windows, while the windows to the terrace and garden are a floor-to-ceiling glass screen.

**e** Standardized components: the standard concrete floor pad containing heating pipes eliminated the need for bulky radiators, while board-and-batten surfaces made plastering redundant. Such innovations achieved affordability and speed of construction.

Built to a two by four foot rectangular module, this grid is incised on the red-colored concrete floor containing the pipes for gravity heating that formed such an essential and economic feature of the standard Usonian. The use of organic materials such as concrete, brick, and wood paneling both integrated the house more closely to its site and had the practical effect of absorbing the noise of children's activity in the communal areas of the house which take up a third of the available interior space. The Jacobs House has an "L" shaped plan, with the communal and quiet spaces of the house joined at an angle of 90 degrees, while there is an inner sanctum or study area at the topmost tip of the "L."

Externally, too, the Jacobs House reflected Wright's radical rethinking of the place of the family house in changing times. The Prairie houses had presented an affluent public face and a clearly defined entrance to the street, often with sparkling displays of art-glass windows, while the Californian textile block houses of the 20s, which were often built on seemingly inaccessible sites presented a fortress-like appearance. The floor-to-ceiling windows of the Jacobs House face the interior of the lot and a modest entrance and clerestory windows ensure privacy on the street side. This idea of "shelter in the open" had been propounded by Wright in 1931: the modern family house had no need to "box up or hole in," as "security in every sense" was to be found in "free wide spacing and integral construction...Spaciousness is for safety as well as for beauty."

In 1956 Herbert Jacobs, who worked as a reporter for *Capital Times* for 26 years recalled his family's experience of the house. "The temptation is to be together much more...I think it does something to you subconsciously. I think it did something to my children...Living in that house was fantastically wonderful."

Herbert and Katherine Jacobs were so delighted with their house that they commissioned Wright to build a second residence for them at Middleton, Wisconsin, in 1944. This took the form of a two-story solar hemicycle with the bedrooms on an upper level.

LEFT: Corner of living room, with windows to the terrace on the left. Different zones are provided within the multipurpose open space of the living room for varying activities. The alcove shown could be used for quiet activities and is provided with purpose built shelving and table space. It is lit from above by the continuous line of clerestory windows, which form the most distinctive feature of the public façade of the house.

RIGHT: Exterior view with entrance. As with other early Usonians, the Jacobs House presented an open and closed façade, which differentiated the private and public aspects of the building. The façade on the private side of the house seen here is open in aspect with extensive ranges of floor-to-ceiling windows. The horizontality of the "L"-shaped plan is marked, as is the use of economical materials such as brick and lapped wood paneling.

# BAZETT HOUSE

**Sidney Bazett (Bazett-Frank) House**
**Constructed:** 1939
**Address:** 101, Reservoir Road, Hillsborough, California 94010.

Like its predecessor, the Hanna House, Wright's second house in the San Francisco area was built on a hexagonal module. It is a compact variant on the "diagonal plan," a version of the first and most common type of Usonian, the inline "T" or "L" shaped plan which had originally been built on a rectangular module, as in the Jacobs House. After the success of the Hanna or Honeycomb House, begun some three years previously, Wright continued to explore the possibilities of the hexagonal shape as he believed that the hexagonal module offered greater spatial freedom than the rectangle of the previous Usonians.

From his earliest designs in the 1880s, Wright had been concerned in "breaking the box" of the conventional domestic space and was convinced that the hexagon and, eventually and logically, the circle was more natural and "organic" in terms of human movement. Certainly in comparing the Jacobs House to the Hanna House there is an entirely different feeling for external and internal space. The Hanna House walls and axes are at 60 and 120 degree angles and the same is true of the Bazett house, although it is more compact and Wright altered and expanded it from its original conception for later owners.

The house itself was relatively small in its original form, measuring 1,500 square feet to accommodate Sidney and Louise Bazett's original specification of their needs and their modest budget of $7,000. The Bazett's had been attracted by the Usonian ideal of a design for convenience, economy, and

RIGHT: Living room interior. Although compact in size, less than 1,500 square feet, the Bazett House is so ingeniously designed that it appears more spacious and expansive. The living room has a high ceiling and the continuous run of perforated panels that form a clerestory at ceiling height throw interesting patterns of sunlight into the room. The floor-to-ceiling windows and doors onto the terrace form what is virtually a glass curtain.

comfort and greatly admired the Hanna House. In the event, the costs of building rose steeply at a time of economic depression and the family lived in the house for only six years while declaring themselves pleased with the finished result after successfully negotiating the changes they needed with Wright.

The next occupants were Betty and Lou Frank who required more room for their growing family and Wright progressively modified the original design, adding first a playroom cum studio and extending the number of bedrooms to four, thus ingeniously increasing the living space despite the original house's relatively small size and compactness. The flexibility of the Usonian plan and, especially of the use of the hexagonal module, was amply demonstrated and the house was completed in its present form in the mid-50s.

The most distinctive internal feature of the house is still the original living room space which is joined to the bedroom wing at an angle of 60 degrees. As the room is set, it commands a view of the valley and the bay in the distance as well as views out onto the terrace and into the "L" of the inward looking space. The distinctive floor-to-ceiling fenestration takes the form of an angled glass curtain wall, while more light is diffused through a series of clerestory windows of a unique design formed of fretwork redwood batten. The same redwood is used throughout the house for walls and ceilings and for built-in furnishing. The focal point of the living space is a large angled brick fireplace of distinctive design.

Externally the house is distinguished by the gables of its roof, which were adapted from the original design as the Bazetts wished to have a roof that would be appropriate for the Californian climate. Wright, perhaps looking back to the Prairie houses of the first period of his success in domestic design, provided steep overhangs, which cast deep shadows and offer protection from bright light. The surrounding landscaped area has repeating hexagonal motifs in the form of plant tubs, mirroring those on the terraces, while the carport, which was so essential a feature of the Usonian principle is double-width to contain two cars.

PREVIOUS PAGES: Exterior of the house, looking into the "L.". The Bazett House is built on a hexagonal module like its predecessor in the San Francisco area, the Hanna House. Although its module is different, it still follows the Usonian "L" principle with the bedroom wing joined to the living and dining areas at an angle of 60 degrees. The Bazett House is both more modest and compact than the Hanna House and was built more economically.

LEFT: Exterior of living room. The ingenious plan of the Bazett House and its careful positioning on the site allows its living room windows to face both into the "L" of its construction on one side and out into the valley and bay beyond on the opposite side. The broad overhang of the eaves here protects what is virtually a glass curtain of windows against extremes of sunlight.

RIGHT: Interior of living room, with terrace beyond. Built-in furniture and storage was an essential part of the Usonian home and clients were invited by Wright to state their preferences in this, as in other key areas of the design. Here a continuous run of built-in seating is topped by a run of shelving and display space beneath the band of clerestory windows. The filtered light from above provides perfect lighting for the artworks and family possessions beneath.

# GOETSCH-WINCKLER HOUSE

**Alma Goetsch and Katherine Winckler House**
**Constructed:** 1939
**Address:** Okemos, Michigan.

Alma Goetsch and Katherine Winckler were both art teachers, who first met as colleagues on the Michigan State College campus in 1928. Two years later, Wright was invited to lecture to students and mount an exhibition of his work at the college and the women were among many in the college community inspired by his ideas. Wright was a compelling lecturer and enjoyed addressing young people. "They all feel," he wrote after one of his lecture tours, "that what grandmother had and the way grandmother had it was all right because grandmother was all right, but not just the thing for them now. And that applies to buildings just as much or even more than anything else."

Alma Goetsch and Katherine Winckler were part of a progressive group of educators working at Michigan State College in the 30s and 40s who formed part of a larger Humanist movement. The two women were instrumental in setting up the Okemos Usonia group which formed a cooperative in order to purchase land in Okemos. On this site the group wished to build their community, inspired by the Wrightian ideas expressed in his writings and lectures and, in particular, by the founding of the Taliesin Fellowship and his proposed plan for Broadacre City. Recalling the spirit and plans of the group of seven, a surviving member wrote that they were "incandescent with the idea of having these Usonian Homes" which were to form a community built around a farm on a 40 acre plot. This pooling of resources was intended to overcome the common lack of finance for land purchase available to the intending Usonian owner. By their very nature, the middle-income professionals who were the clients for the early Usonians had little means and had, certainly

RIGHT: Dining area of the living room. The plan of the house offered maximum flexibility in the use of its spaces, not least in the design of the living room, which could double as a studio space for the two art teachers. The dining table backs onto the central fireplace with its secluded seating area beyond. The rectangular unit of the house design is scored into the concrete floor and echoed in the shape of the casement windows, which frame views of the surrounding trees, creating an interior of harmony and elegance.

by 1939 when times were hard, to finance their homes through family savings or independent funds. Wright homes were perceived to be high risk undertakings at the time, and Goetsch and Winckler and other faculty members were unable to obtain a mortgage from their employers, as the journalist Loren Pope had done from *The Washington Star.*

The members of the group shared Wright's hope that after the Depression a cooperative and democratic model of land ownership might replace urbanization and return people to the land. As it happened, the Federal Housing Administration (FHA) refused to finance the loans for the community of houses and only the Goetsch Winckler House was built.

Katherine Winckler wrote to Wright of their then circumstances, "we have a combined income of $4,500 a year and now pay $60.00 a month for the uncertain privilege of manipulating a few gadgets in a so-called four room apartment...We should appreciate enough space so that we could relax at the table without jabbing someone in the ribs with our elbows." Alma Goetsch had "a few qualms about moving into the country," and in a postscript to the joint specification of needs sent to Wright she asked him to "make my bedroom give me a feeling of security." On the other hand Katherine Winckler had admired the fenestration of the Jacobs House bedrooms, "All my life I have resented the little holes in walls that people call windows and as I stood (there)... I realized what it must mean to step out of bed in the morning and see earth and trees and sky all at once."

In order to achieve the desires of both clients, Wright planned that the central living space which also doubled as a studio, should be higher than the bedroom wing, entrance gallery, kitchen workspace, and alcove. In these latter areas where privacy was essential, strips of clerestory windows provide light, while as in other Usonians, the central placing of the kitchen workspace enabled anyone working there to command a view of the living area. An alcove, beside the central fireplace with its open fire, takes on the function of the traditional inglenook providing a secluded space, while the flexible open living space functions as a studio providing both the necessary social and study spaces for two academics in this house without children.

In plan, the Goetsch-Winckler House is a single line Usonian built on a four foot square module. As with the other houses, heat comes from below, the maze of hot water pipes in the concrete base provided such efficient heating that the windows could be left slightly open even in winter, providing the airflow that both the owners and Wright considered a vital circumstance. Wright stressed the importance of "thorough protection overhead and the rest of the building as open to the breezes as it is possible can be made."

ABOVE: Exterior view. The concrete, redwood, and brick construction is surmounted by no less than three levels of flat, cantilevered roofs, which appear to float above the structure, an effect enhanced by the continuous band of clear clerestory windows which reflect the surrounding trees and provide light from above, throughout the interior. The horizontal emphasis of the building is marked and it appears anchored by the broad rectangular chimney.

RIGHT: Exterior view. The cantilevered roofs at different levels provide a dramatic roof-line to the in-line plan of this early Usonian design. The carport is particularly startling as it projects some 18 feet from the workspace which provides its support. Unusually, the workspace and fireplace are at the end of the house, behind the carport and a more intimate space is created around the broad chimney breast and hearth.

# ROSENBAUM HOUSE

**Stanley and Mildred Rosenbaum House**
**Constructed:** 1939
**Address:** 601 Riverview Drive, Florence, Alabama 35630.
The house is under renovation at the time of writing and is not open to the public except by special appointment. It will be opened in 2002.

On their marriage in 1938, Professor Stanley Rosenbaum and his wife Mildred were recommended to seek Wright as their architect by a mutual friend, Aaron Green, who had studied at Taliesin and was later to work with Wright on several projects in the San Francisco area. In many ways they, like Alma Goetsch and Katherine Winckler (who were also academics), were the ideal Usonian clients. Wright described the would-be Usonian owners who sought him out at this period as "A cross-section of the distinctly better type of American, I should say Usonian, to be more specific—most of them with an aesthetic sense of their own, many of them artistic, accomplished, and most of them traveled. They (are)…people who are rich in other things than money. It seems as though the appreciation of our work is inversely proportioned to the financial standing of the person involved."

In plan, the Rosenbaum House, which is set in two acres of land, is a variant on the basic Usonian "L" shape, and is built of cypress and brick on a rectangular module. The house, which is 1,540 square foot, is closed and protected on the public side and opens onto the landscape and the Tennessee River beyond on the family side of the house. The street façade presents itself with three roof layers above the brick and wood walls, with only thin strips of clerestory windows as fenestration, and these are set deep in the shadow of the roof projections. The two wings of the house enclose a raised garden to the south, and this is subtly integrated with the living area by the extension of the concrete pad supporting the house at the innermost corner of the

RIGHT: View of the living room with dining area beyond. The distinctive cut-out design of the clerestory windows diffuses the light above the extensive run of floor-to-ceiling windows and doors opening onto the terrace. The pierced fretwork pattern of the clerestory windows is repeated on the opposite of the room in the illuminated ceiling panels set to the left of the hearth and above the dining room, seen in the distance on the right-hand side of the room.

"L." The two by four foot grid that forms the module of the entire structure is marked out on the concrete both internally and externally, thus, literally, in Wright's words "bringing the outside in."

At the heart of the house, beyond the entry is the workspace, while one wing of the "L" contains three bedrooms and two baths. The other includes a spacious living room and library, with a reading table, as well as the quintessential Wrightian fireplace and fireplace alcove, providing a secluded space almost akin to the inglenook around the "sacred hearth," as Wright was to term it in the earlier houses. Indeed this essential element of Wright's domestic architecture, which is a key feature of his own house at Oak Park of 1889 and forms the axis of the pinwheel design of Wingspread, built for Herbert F. Johnson in 1937—which Wright considered his finest and most expensive house—takes on a new life in the Usonian houses.

Wright conceived the "sacred hearth" as symbolizing the focus of family life, an essential contact with a necessity of life. Gravity heat rose through the floor pad of the Usonian house providing essential background warmth, while a living flame remains at the heart of the home. This focus remained when the house was extended to a "T"-shape to provide bedrooms for the Rosenbaum's four sons and a courtyard addition.

Floor-to-ceiling windows bring the outside inside visually on the family side of the house in nearly all the room spaces, while providing access to the terraces and landscaping beyond. As with other Usonian houses, there is a strong sense of horizontality, of the house being at one with its site, a feeling enhanced by the distinctive patterns of the fretwork clerestory window strips on the closed side of the house.

RIGHT, ABOVE: View of the exterior on the family side of the house from the terrace. Like other Usonian houses of the period, in the Rosenbaum House, the family side of the dwelling opens onto the landscape from a series of floor-to-ceiling windows and French doors. This applies to the bedrooms as well as to the living room, which all open onto terraces and landscaping beyond. The Rosenbaum House was extended in 1948 to accommodate the growing family.

RIGHT: View of dining area with the hearth beyond. As in other early Usonians, the dining area is contained in an area that is part of, yet offset from the living room, opening onto the workspace, which is to the left. Wright designed the built-in cypress shelving and storage space. The wood is also used for the ceiling and the distinctive pierced fretwork panels set into the ceiling which provide illumination from above into the otherwise dimly lit space.

The distinctive pierced panel design of the clerestory windows is repeated in the continuous run of illuminated light screens set into the boards of the ceiling. The lighting of the interior of the Rosenbaum House is particularly subtle, making maximum use of natural light at different levels and helping to articulate the private and social spaces of the house, creating a series of changing "vistas within" in Wright's terms. The house is built on Wright's preferred southerly orientation, and the marked horizontality of the design appears to ground the house as an integral part of its site. In Wright's words in *The Natural House* published in 1954, "I see this extended horizontal line as the true earth line of human life, indicative of freedom. Always."

The house, which was built for $12,000, proved adaptable to the changing needs of the Rosenbaum family and in 1978 was put into the *National Register of Historic Places.* Mildred Wright was honored by the Frank Lloyd Wright Building Conservancy in 1991, with one of the first Wright Spirit Awards in recognition of her expertise and the fact that she had maintained her house longer than any other single owner.

RIGHT: Bathroom of Rosenbaum House. The Rosenbaum House contained three bathrooms. The extensions of 1948, which provided another gallery and a dormitory for the sons of the family also included the addition of a bathroom for the exclusive use of the master bedroom as well as a guest room with its own separate bathroom. The spaces are lit from above by skylights and are paneled in cypress throughout.

# POPE LEIGHEY HOUSE

**Loren B. Pope (Pope Leighey) House**
**Address:** Woodlawn Plantation, 9000 Richmond Highway (US 1 & Route 235)
Alexandria, Virginia.
Tours available

Like Herbert Jacobs, owner of the first Usonian to be built, Loren Pope was a journalist. He worked for the *Washington Evening Star* and, in August 1939, he wrote to Wright with a request which brought a ready response for a "Jacobs-style house" and one, moreover, that would be affordable on a salary of $50 a week: "There are certain things a man wants during life, and, of life. Material things and things of the spirit...one fervent wish...includes both. It is for a house created by you." By November that same year plans for an L-shaped Usonian structure built on the identical two by four foot rectangular module to that of the Jacobs House were completed, for the house to be built on a site in Falls Church, Virginia. The Loren and Charlotte Pope House was smaller than that built for the Jacobs family—some 1,200 square feet rather than 1,340 and cost $8,000 to construct by the time it was completed in 1941.

Wright believed strongly in the precise orientation of his buildings: "The sun is the great luminary of all life. It should serve as such in the building of any house." Especially important was the southern orientation of the living room elevation which faced the garden, and here the living room space is open on both sides, thus bringing the "outdoors in" to an even greater degree than that of the Jacobs House. The house, of wood,

RIGHT: View of the main living area, looking toward the hearth with the dining area beyond. The wooden fretwork panels are here used horizontally to provide a continuous band of clerestory windows at ceiling height. These panels, in the same distinctive cut-out pattern as those used throughout the house as a unifying design motif, serve a dual function as clerestory windows, both filtering the light into the interior and providing a series of continuous frames at ceiling height through which to view the trees of the surrounding plantation.

brick, and glass with the brick fireplace and workspace at its heart was, like the Jacobs House, built to such a flexible and efficient design that the whole structure could be removed and rebuilt on its present site when threatened by the building of an interstate highway in 1964. Its second owner, Mrs Marjorie Leighey, donated it to the National Trust for Historic Preservation and it was reassembled at its present historic site at Woodlawn Plantation in 1965 on a different orientation to that originally intended.

A distinctive feature of the Pope Leighey House is the use of plywood light-screens which form an integral part of the design. The play of light through such wooden screens is a characteristic Wrightian device, he had used perforated panels with abstract motifs in the Californian textile block houses in the 1920s. Clerestory windows are formed of horizontal fretwork cut-outs which frame views of the surrounding trees. The same abstract cut-out motifs are used singly or in pairs vertically to form perforated panels of Cherokee red

RIGHT: Although modest in size, with only two bedrooms, the Popes had specified among their requirements the necessity of a quiet space in which to work away from the bustle of family life. As in other early Usonians, the Pope Leighey House was provided with an inner sanctum or study, in this case in a quiet area to one side of the entry. Here the distinctive cut-out wooden panels are used vertically rather than horizontally to offset the horizontal emphasis seen elsewhere in the design.

joinery—a material used throughout the building, which helps create a simple yet highly effective organic whole. The cut-out devices in both horizontal and vertical panels cast interesting shadows in this and other Usonians, a feature long remembered by those who lived in them.

The Pope Leighey House is one of only three Wright Houses in the care of the National Trust and is open to the public.

LEFT: Exterior of living room with fretwork screen on the left. The Pope Leighey House is built on different levels with the living and dining areas on a slight slope down from the entry level. This serves to further integrate the building to its site. The broad overhangs, so typical of Usonian houses, emphasize the ground-hugging qualities deemed so essential by Wright to the concept of "shelter in the open." The Pope Leighey House offsets this horizontality by using occasional vertical elements such as this fretwork screen, while openings in the roof over the windows offset the breadth of the overhangs and let in the light.

ABOVE: View of the exterior of the living room with screened porch. The house when first built in Falls Church, Virginia, was distinctive among the early Usonians in several respects, not least in its use of wood. The construction used a two by four foot rectangular module and employed extensive areas of sunk-batten paneling. The wood used was true bald cypress, Taxodium distichum. The lightness and flexibility of this mode of construction contributed in no small measure to its relocation in 1964.

# WALTER HOUSE

**Lowell and Agnes Walter House "Cedar Rock"**
**Constructed:** 1948–50
**Address:** 2611 Quasqueton Diag. Boulevard, Quasqueton, Iowa.
**Tours:** May through October. Two evening showings, June and October.

Wright called the Walter House his "Opus 497," an indication of the number of works he had produced up until 1945 when the design was first completed. The house was built as a retirement home on a farmland site on part of a limestone bluff in a bend of the Wapsipincon River, owned by Lowell Walter's family for generations. Wright's knowledge of the Midwest was in itself a recommendation to Lowell Walter, who had sold his road building company in 1944, but because of wartime building restrictions the house could not begin building until 1948. More than 50 years later it survives almost intact with the majority of the interior fixtures and fittings designed by Wright in original condition, thanks to a trust fund set up in 1981 on Walter Lowell's death and is now maintained by the Iowa Department of National Resources. The 11 acre site, which is entered by iron gates designed by Wright, contains the house itself, a two-story river pavilion which also serves as a boathouse, and an outdoor hearth with a low surrounding wall known as the "Council Fire" on a knoll above the house. Wright's initials are embedded in the entranceway of the house as a mark of his close involvement in the design throughout.

The house has a reinforced concrete roof and floors, and follows Usonian principles to a marked degree. However, a generous budget for both house and fixtures renders the space far more spacious and expensively appointed than usual and it is built on a spectacular site in a wooded valley that would be beyond the means of the average Usonian owner. The building materials are again beyond the reach of the average

RIGHT: View of the interior of the garden room, the major living room space of the house. The room measures some 900 square feet while the fireplace (in the background on the right) holds logs which can be up to five feet in length. The pierced skylights of the concrete roof and the continuous run of clerestory windows, filled with clear glass without the usual Usonian pierced patterns, help flood the space with light from above.

Usonian client: thick masonry walls combine with red-brick, steel, and walnut. Integral gravity heating is used in the foundation slab as in other Usonians. However, in order to deal with any problems that might arise in the system, the heating units are laid in independent segments, so that any fault could be immediately located and dealt with. This system is unique to the house. Again, most Usonians were designed to be run without servants, but in this house there are separate maid's quarters which, together with a storage space for tools, are separated from the house by the carport.

In form, the house is a variant on the "L" plan, or "pollywog" as Wright termed it, but with the living and dining area, here aptly termed the garden room, set diagonally against the bedroom wing with the workspace in the pivotal position off the main entry.

Based on a square, five-foot, three-inch module, the exterior of the house is distinguished by a reinforced concrete roof with broad cantilevered overhangs with upturned edges which are pierced as a form of trellis. This has the effect of shading the extensive areas of window glass from bright sunlight and

RIGHT: Exterior of the house from the river side. The steep overhang of the reinforced concrete roof is lightened by pierced square forms which echo those of the skylights in the roof which surmount the garden room. Each of the sets of openings serve both to lighten the structure and to allow the maximum amount of daylight to reach the interior of the garden room. The extensive terracing is also lavishly planted.

providing the main feature, the garden room, which has three glass walls and a series of skylights, with sufficient continuous daylight for the growth of a sizeable interior garden built into the concrete floor and provided with constant heat from the gravity system of the floor slab. This feature is unique in Wright's domestic work, although it is a marked characteristic of his public buildings such as the Marin County Civic Center. The windows provide spectacular views, appearing to dissolve the barrier between internal and external space, while at night, recessed artificial light creates the effect of daylight.

The spectacular space is some 900 feet in area, and as an indication of the scale of the room, the fireplace, which gives it focus, can hold five foot logs. Wright designed much of the built-in and the freestanding furniture. Walnut is used throughout, from the waxed walnut shelves to the specially designed seating, which can be moved to form different combinations.

The two-story river pavilion, further down the site, is designed as a boathouse with its own floating pier and a roomy retreat cum sun terrace above. Wright designed the building to mirror the house above it, especially in the material of its construction. There is a reinforced concrete roof above the retreat, which is served by a pantry and screened porch as well as extensive sun terracing.

# PALMER HOUSE

**William and Mary Palmer House**
**Constructed:** 1950
**Address:** 227 Orchard Hills Drive, Ann Arbor, Michigan 48104.

William Palmer was a professor at the University of Michigan and as a boy in California had been taken to see the Alice Millard House, "La Miniatura" by his grandfather. The concrete textile block house was Palmer's introduction to the work of Frank Lloyd Wright, recalled when he and his wife Mary decided to build.

Like the Hagans who built on Kentuck Knob in Pennsylvania, the couple had chosen a hilly site near the campus where William Palmer worked, and sought to familiarize themselves with Wright's philosophy before commissioning the house.

The house plan is in-line in form and based on an equilateral triangle with the carport set below the main house on the hill at an angle of 120 degrees. The original plan had the main living area as south-facing but this proved awkward for the site and it was reoriented to fit the ridge at an angle 120 degrees to the northeast. As with the Hagan House, the Palmer House appears integrated with the hillside: the deep overhang of the eaves, and brick walls and terraces render it one of Wright's most successful enterprises in wedding a building to its site.

The setting up of the visitor's expectations on approaching the entrance to the house, which was a consistent feature of Wright's buildings from the 1890s onward, is here achieved by concealing the entry,

RIGHT: Entrance seen from the terrace. The entrance to the Palmer House is concealed in a manner familiar from earlier houses in Wright's career. A flight of shallow steps constructed from the custom-made block leads from the terrace to a narrow entrance way which opens into the lofty interior. Thus, the building achieves an effect of compression and then of expansion once the interior is gained.

as in the Frank Thomas House at Oak Park of 1901 for example, to achieve a sense of mystery and spatial compression. The effect of entering the spacious living room from such an entrance is thus heightened, and the triangularity of the whole concept is revealed. The dramatic nature of the exterior is further enhanced by the extraordinarily extended projection of the triangular point of the prow-like roof which shelters the terrace, itself conceived as a natural extension of the building.

The geometric nature of the building is further enhanced by the huge rectangular chimney stack serving the main hearth at the heart of the house. Wright had experimented with geometric forms from his earliest days as an architect, being influenced, as he writes in the *Autobiography* and elsewhere, by the Froebel system of wooden teaching blocks given him as a child by his mother. Wright asserted that he learned the fundamental laws of nature through the blocks and their shapes may be seen throughout his work. In the Palmer House, the essential horizontality of the building on its ridge is set off by the acute angles of the triangular roof while it appears seemingly anchored to its site by the massive rectangular chimney, a device reminiscent of that used in Wright's first independent commission, the Winslow House in River Forest, Illinois, of 1893.

A second, smaller triangle forms the bedroom wing, which also contains the study and bathrooms, reached by a narrow, galley-like passage. The geometric nature of the building is further emphasized by the grid scored in the concrete floor of the living space. This device had been used in the earliest Usonians, and here the red waxed floor is incised with parallelograms. The shapes and coloration are echoed in the red tidewater boards that form the ceiling. Both the sand-mold brick and the block that form the house are from the

RIGHT: Exterior view of house and terrace. The Palmer House is set on the crest of a hill at different levels, with its carport at the lowest level and set at 20 degrees to the main axis of the triangular building. The steeply raked roof with an exceptionally broad overhang is also triangular and made of cypress. The roof covers the spacious living and dining area of the house and is mirrored in the terrace which leads from the living room. The apex of the triangle on the ground is formed by a large brick planter.

same manufacturer and are fired in the same way. Wright had long sought such consistency of building material, and the "Cranbrook brick," so-called because it was used by the famous Finnish architect, Eliel Saarinen for his Cranbrook Academy buildings, together with the block and the red tones of the wood used throughout the house and of the stained floor, help give the building its remarkable unity.

The living room built-in units are also of cypress and the elegant simplicity and harmony of the house is complemented by the range of Japanese textiles and artifacts. The Palmers shared Wright's lifelong passion for Japanese design and the sense of calm and repose that is associated with it, and this is evident both inside and out, most markedly, perhaps in the Japanese-inspired garden.

Unlike most other Usonian houses, the Palmer House has been in its original owners' possession since it was built, ageing gracefully over more than half a century. In 1964, the addition of a garden or tea-house which mirrors the triangular shape of the original building was built lower down the slope of the hill by John H. Howe, who had worked as an associate with Wright on the house itself.

RIGHT: View of terrace from living room. Built-in seating is a feature of Usonian design. In the Palmer House this extends to the seating on the terrace which is constructed from cypress in keeping with the timber used throughout the house. The fine detailing of the triangular roof is carried through in the triangular forms incised in the concrete floor.

# ZIMMERMAN HOUSE

**Lucille and Isadore J. Zimmerman House**
**Constructed:** 1950
**Address:** 201 Myrtle Way, Manchester, New Hampshire 03104.
**Tours:** From the Currier gallery of Art, 192 Orange Street, Manchester, NH.

Dr Zimmerman and his wife wanted this Usonian design to express their lifestyle, central to which was their love of music and its performance. Consequently the house is designed around the main living area, which in this instance also doubled as a concert space for the Zimmermans and their musical friends. The house is designed on a four foot square unit module and is long and spacious, constructed on an in-line plan with, unusually, the bedrooms situated around the workspace and an interior space of 1,458 square feet.

The Zimmermans had no children and had sought Wright's help in designing their ideal home after reading his *Autobiography*. Although the site was too far distant from Taliesin East or West for Wright to supervise the building and fitting of the house himself, the design of much of the interior fixtures and fittings was directed by him in close consultation with the Zimmermans, with whom he shared many interests, especially music. As with other Usonian houses, an apprentice from Taliesin was assigned under Wright's instruction as site supervisor while other apprentices worked on the details of furniture and furnishings, which in this case, apparently extended to the design of soft furnishings. There were several unique design features including the illuminated quartet stand which is based on one specially designed for use at Taliesin and formed a distinctive focus of the Zimmermans' musical gatherings.

The close collaboration between Wright and his clients is shown by the fact that the site supervisor appointed from Taliesin, John Geiger, unusually boarded with the couple while working on their home. The

RIGHT: Exterior view of the Zimmerman House showing the distinctive design of the keyhole windows, which are set high on the brick base of the building on the public side of the house. The windows run the length of the street façade of the house on either side of the entrance, ensuring privacy and providing a "closed" aspect under the broad overhang of the roof, in contrast to the extensive fenestration of the private side.

resulting house was particularly elegant in its integrated detail, while the red-glazed brick and flat terra-cotta tile of the roof, allied to the choice of upland Georgia cypress trim give the entire building a warmth and rectilinear quality which is reminiscent of the earlier Prairie houses, an effect enhanced by the low roof lines and masonry walls.

An addition to the usual Usonian concrete floor pad with the all-essential heating pipes which provided the gravity heating for the house, was the use of a patented material, Colorundum, which was placed in a water-repellent layer on top of the foundation pad of the house. Colorundrum could be made available in a choice of colors, rather than the red stain which had been added to the concrete base of the earliest Usonians. Wright was always ready to embrace new technologies from his earliest commissions, and saw the new material as the solution to the problem of flooring large uncarpeted areas with underfloor heating.

RIGHT: View of the interior of the living room. The house is designed around the main living area which doubled as a concert space, as the love of music and its performance was central to the lives of Dr. Zimmerman and his wife. The distinctive clerestory windows are contrasted with the facing range of large square windows giving directly onto the terrace. The specially designed quartet music stand is a copy of one at Taliesin.

The terrace opening from the dining area is oriented to the southwest to gain maximum sunlight. The dissolution of the barriers between interior and exterior on the garden side of the living room is achieved in a unique form. Within the room, the four floor-to-ceiling square windows are set in bays between brick piers that look directly onto the terrace and the surrounding landscape. The dissolution of the barrier between "the vista without" and "the vista within" as Wright termed it, is enhanced by the fact that the lower pane of fixed glass connects to a continuous length of planting boxes at floor level. This feature is mirrored on the terrace side, thus serving Wright's governing principle of "bringing the outside in." Above this, the central window frame itself is set into flanking fixed panes of glass, and, to create an unbroken line, is fixed directly to the cypress ceiling boards, an element of the design that is further reinforced below by the fact that the fixed side panes (only the square windows open) are set directly into the wood on one side and into brick on the other, thus forming a triptych of windows.

The living, or garden room, as it is termed on the plans, is 36 feet long and the range of floor-to-ceiling windows that form virtually a wall of glass onto the terrace and the wooded landscape beyond is set in sharp contrast to the opposite side of the room which opens out onto the street. Here, in a feature reminiscent

of the closed nature of the California textile block houses, some thirty years before, Wright ensures the privacy of the occupants with a distinctive design motif. Keyhole windows formed of perforated and glazed concrete blocks are placed high on the brick base of the building.

LEFT: House marker and postbox on Myrtle Way. Many of the exterior and interior details of the Zimmerman House are unique, including some of the furnishings and the accommodation made for Dr. and Mrs. Zimmerman's musical interests, which Wright shared. The house marker and postbox are designed to form a miniature replica of the distinctive roof line of the structure and are made of the same materials, brick and cypress, as the house itself.

ABOVE: Exterior of house on the terrace side. The living room of the Zimmerman House is distinguished by its unique range of windows, from the concrete block keyhole windows on the street side to the four square window bays seen here on the left. The lower fixed panes connect to a continuous length of planting boxes, a feature mirrored on the terrace side, a feature unique in Wright's domestic work.

# HAGAN HOUSE

**I.N. Hagan house (Kentuck Knob)**
**Constructed:** 1954
**Address:** Ohiopyle Road , Chalkhill, Pennsylvania 15421.
Tours available

Isaac Newton Hagan ran the family dairy business in Uniontown and had commissioned an ice-cream company building from Wright, which was unrealized. Edgar Kauffmann, Sr., owner of the famous Fallingwater not far from Uniontown, was a business associate. I.N. Hagan and his wife, Bernardine, admired Wright's work and wished to commission a house on a spectacular 79 acre site purchased in 1953, not far from Fallingwater. While not wishing for as radical a design as Edgar Kauffmann's (to whom I.N. Hagan expressed his admiration in the following terms "with each subsequent visit this great house of yours becomes more entrancing to us"), the Hagans desired a similar organic unity between structure and site.

At Wright's suggestion they visited several of his buildings, including the Herbert Jacobs House and the Usonian House Exhibition in New York City while discussing their plans with the architect. The Hagans also visited and much admired a very different building, the Unitarian Meeting House at Shorewood Hills, Wisconsin, which had been essentially completed in 1951. The Unitarian Meeting House uses local stone, with a distinctive copper roof and is built to a plan of a diamond module with 60 and 120 degree angles. Elements from this diversity of sources were incorporated into the Hagan House, giving an unusual and luxurious dimension to the usual Usonian components such as the pivotal workspace, focal open hearth, and clerestory windows.

RIGHT: View from the courtyard. The roughly cut stone of the walls is laid as a facing on the retaining walls of the entire structure which are made of concrete, containing dirt and fill for the solid construction of the podium under the main floor of the house. The Hagan House is remarkable for the solidity of its structure and its use of costly materials. The walls at ground level are ten inches thick and above this there are double walls of stone with insulation laid between.

The module for the entire house was a four foot six inch equilateral parallelogram, and the complex geometry of the plan contains hexagons and subsidiary triangles. However, unlike the early Usonian houses, where the unit of planning was incised on the concrete floor, clearly expressing the unity of form and function, the Hagan House conceals its design beneath a variety of floor coverings, notably with stone cladding in the living and dining area and the workspace with cork tile.

The workspace is illuminated by a skylight and opens both to the entry hall and the dining area which, like the living area, was made larger than the usual Usonian plan at the Hagan's request by the simple expedient of increasing the number of modules. The orientation of the house is such that winter sunshine reaches the flagstone floor (specified by the Hagans as one of the features adapted from Fallingwater) while it is excluded in summer.

RIGHT: Exterior from below. The house is sited immediately south of Kentuck Knob rather than on the more obvious and less challenging site on top of the hill. The house thus appears to be an organic and harmonious part of its site, essentially visually integrated with it, rather than dominating it, while the triangular living room space topped by its dramatic copper roof, appears like a landlocked ship's prow in the clearing among the trees, and evokes the inspiration for its design, Wright's Unitarian Church.

Masonry is an important feature of the house. The retaining walls are of concrete with facings of split sandstone taken from the site itself. This provided excellent insulation while the undressed sandstone weathered to gray with the years to blend with the wood of the trim, which is of Tidewater cypress. The Hagans were persuaded by Wright to use plate glass rather than the insulated material they had originally specified. The architect asserted that the patented material did not have the required transparency to maintain the all-essential connection between the vista within and the spectacular view. The living room is topped by a magnificent copper roof, reminiscent of its design origin, the roof of the Unitarian Meeting House, which has been likened to a ship's prow. Even from a distance, the Hagan House seems at one with its site, topped by its dramatic roof line with its wide, pierced overhang, the copper, stone, and wood ageing gracefully to further emphasize the organic nature of the construction and its total harmonization with its site.

The house contains built-in cypress fixtures in key areas, as with other Wright houses, and some of the freestanding furniture commissioned by the Hagans was formed of 60 degree angles to chime with the design of the house, with some of the furniture being designed at Taliesin. Wright's advice was enlisted in the planting of the trees on the mountainous terrain and some 8,000 seedlings formed a forest, which together with extensive landscaping and terracing transformed the site.

The Hagan House, now owned by Lord Palumbo and open to the public, is a unique example of a collaboration between Wright and thoughtful clients, well versed in Wright's ideas. It demonstrates that the principles of Usonian design could be creatively and harmoniously adapted to respond to a challenging and dramatic site. The house, one of the last to be completed by Wright, provides an intriguing contrast with Fallingwater nearby.

RIGHT ABOVE: Dining area with view to the terrace beyond. The dining table is lit from above by a series of triangular glass forms with recessed lights set into the panels of the ceiling. The orientation of the house, as so often with Wright's houses, is to the south and west for the maximum amount of sunlight throughout the year. The living and dining space floors are covered with stone, which provides visual continuity with the outside space of the terrace.

RIGHT BELOW: View of the living room with terrace beyond. The living room of the Hagan House is sited under the dramatic copper roof of the structure with extensive terracing and superb views of the surrounding landscape. The sandstone used throughout the building was native to the site and is split, but not dressed, to give an organic, naturally weathered appearance. Both the stone of the walls and the flagstone of the floors are laid over a concrete base.

# GAZETTEER

---

## CHARLES L. MANSON HOUSE

**Constructed:** 1938
**Address:** 1224 Grand Avenue, Wausau, Wisconsin, 54401.

The Manson House represents one of Wright's early attempts to vary the original "L"-shaped Usonian plan by an experiment in siting the living room diagonally and eliminating the usual right-angle room corners by employing thirty and sixty degree angles. The ceiling heights are also variations on the norm: while maintaining the long low lines of the typical in-line Usonian, the hall is a low ceiling space, while the children's bedrooms have an ingenious dropped ceiling in order to accommodate a low darkroom space above. The small second story accommodates a servant's room as well as the darkroom, and the variation of ceiling height allows a high ceiling in the spacious living and dining room. The original carport has been converted into an additional room.

LEFT: Exterior view. The "L"-shaped plan Usonian was capable of infinite variation. The Manson House was one of the earliest attempts to move away from the standard plan by setting the living room diagonally and varying the ceiling heights throughout the structure. The construction is mostly brick with board-and-batten and the low second story can be seen to the left.

# BERNARD AND FERN SCHWARTZ HOUSE

**Constructed:** 1939
**Address:** 3425 Adams, Two Rivers, Wisconsin, 54241.

The design for this house was originally published in the September 1938 edition of *Life* magazine—an issue almost wholly devoted to Wright's current projects—as suitable "for a family of $5,000-$6,000 Income." The house was built the following year on a spacious site on the East Twin River, which flows into Lake Michigan. The "T" plan, built on a non-standard 42 square inch unit module is ingeniously oriented on the site in order to provide river views without obstruction in both easterly and southerly directions. A two-story building of some 3,000 square feet, the master bedroom is placed at ground level, while instead of a bedroom wing, two further bedrooms and servants' quarters are placed on the opposite side of this second floor. The plan has a large "recreation room" rather than a living room, with a lounge area in addition to the usual workspace and dining area.

ABOVE: Exterior view of living room façade and garden. The two-story dwelling is ingeniously oriented on the site to receive maximum sunlight while commanding views across the surrounding landscape without being obscured by the buildings in the vicinity. The broad terrace of the cypress and brick construction is reached from what is here termed the "recreation room."

# GREGOR S. AND ELIZABETH B. AFFLECK HOUSE

**Constructed:** 1940
**Address:** 1925 N. Woodward Avenue, Bloomfield Hills, Michigan 48013. Owned by the Lawrence Institute of Technology. Guided tours by appointment.

The Affleck House is built on a spectacular site above a ravine and is modeled on Wright's design for his projected Broadacre City "home for sloping ground." The site presented a challenge which was resolved by cantilevering the living room and spacious terrace above the ravine and using a glass-covered loggia, which opens onto the pool below to both separate and connect the bedroom wing with the living room and workspace. The house is built on a four foot square module to a "T" plan, sometimes termed an outside "L," with basement workshop and utility rooms and accommodation for a servant. Materials of construction include ship-lap cypress siding, a feature unique to the house, and finely finished hard-burned brick.

   The house has been restored by the Lawrence Institute of Technology to whom it was gifted by the Affleck family.

ABOVE: Detail of loggia. The cypress siding is laid in ship-lap fashion, the color of the wood complemented by the choice of hard-burned shale brick. The loggia and broad terrace, together with the use of Wright's favored outward-opening casement windows provide changing views of the wooded site at treetop level.

RIGHT: Exterior view showing the harmonious siting of the house within its woodland setting. The house, which measures some 2,350 square feet is larger than many Usonians and has particularly fine craftsmanly detail. The overlapping cypress siding boards which conceal the standard sandwich walls, emphasize the horizontality of the house and its unity with its setting.

# STUART RICHARDSON HOUSE

**Constructed:** 1940
**Address:** 63 Chestnut Hill Pl. Glen Ridge, New Jersey 07028.

The original Richardson House plan, which was intended to be built at Livingston, is an early instance of Wright's triangular forms, seen at its most innovative in the equilateral triangle of the living cum dining room. The plan was executed in 1951 on a nearby site at Glen Ridge. Wright reoriented the original plan so that the house would benefit from winter sun in the major living spaces, which are lit by floor-to-ceiling glass doors with clerestory windows above. The module on which it is built is also unusual, being hexagonal with 28 inch sides. This entailed the use of specially fired brick with 60 and 120 degree corners to fit the hexagonals. The major construction material is masonry with little use of wood, which is cypress, except in the sloping living room ceiling and in the distinctive cut-outs of the clerestory windows.

ABOVE: Exterior of living room façade, with bedrooms on the right. Triangular forms are used throughout the Richardson House and can be seen here in the corners of the living room space which is constructed from specially manufactured brick. The room is lit from above by clerestory windows in addition to the floor-to-ceiling windows, while at night ceiling lights are used throughout the house.

# ERLING P. AND KATHERINE BRAUNER HOUSE

**Constructed:** 1948
**Address:** 2527 Arrow Head Road, Okemos, Michigan 48864.

The plans for the Brauner House were originally part of the scheme for Wright's "Usonia 1," a community project designed in 1939 to include several Usonian houses designed primarily for teaching staff at Michigan State University. In fact only the Goetsch-Winckler house, which is nearby, was built as part of the original project. After Wright visited the site he devised a second project in consultation with the Brauners, which was an attempt to redefine the Usonian house in terms of concrete block on a four foot square unit module. The usual brick and dry-wall construction is replaced by hollow-core concrete blocks measuring four by eight by 16 inches, giving the house a distinctive appearance, particularly on its "closed" more public side. In plan, the house is a variant on the in-line plan, with the bed and bath rooms sited off a corridor behind the workspace.

ABOVE: Exterior of the house with entryway and carport. The Brauner House is distinguished by its use of double hollow-core concrete block construction which replaces the brick of the standard Usonian house. On the public façade of the house seen here, the pierced blocks provide privacy from the street, the pattern of the perforations is repeated in the front door decoration.

# ROBERT LEVIN HOUSE

**Constructed:** 1948
**Address:** 2816 Taliesin Drive, Kalamazoo, Michigan 49008.

The Levin House is one of the Parkwyn Village houses and is distinguished from the nearby houses by several factors, not least the treatment of its exterior to the southwest. This, the living room façade which opens out onto a screened terrace on one side, has a series of stepped

bays which add variety and interest to both exterior and interior, while maximizing privacy. The house is constructed on different levels, with the workspace and laundry set on a lower level, with a spacious study reached by stairs from the gallery that run along the bedroom wing in the "quiet" part of the house. The house is set on the usual concrete foundation with under-floor gravity heating. This is stained dark tan to complement the sand-colored textile blocks from which the house is constructed. Unlike the other Parkwyn Village houses, the wood used here is red Tidewater cypress, rather than mahogany.

ABOVE: View of south-west façade. Under the broad overhang of the roof the living room of the Levin House opens onto a terrace at one side. The terrace is screened with an iron pipe trellis giving added privacy and shade. In a manner reminiscent of the Prairie houses, the broad overhang of the roof shades the large areas of window glass that form the distinctive bays of the living room.

# ERIC AND PAT PRATT HOUSE

**Constructed:** 1948
**Address:** 11036 Hawthorne Drive, Galesburg, Michigan 49053.

The Pratt House is one of the Galesburg Country Homes, built by an association of friends who achieved huge savings in construction costs by acting as their own contractors and employing group purchasing methods to buy timber that would otherwise be prohibitively expensive. The Pratts made their own concrete textile blocks for the construction of their house and used expensive Honduras mahogany, bought jointly from a Grand Rapids lumber yard and economically milled locally. Both the concrete floor and the wooden elements are stained red. The house is a standard, if lengthier than most, in-line Usonian, with the bedroom wing extended as the family grew. It is constructed on a four foot square module and was built in three stages. The large studio, set to one side of the entry adjacent to the carport, was enlarged by Eric Pratt and served a dual purpose as a workshop.

LEFT: The long, in-line Usonian was constructed from standard concrete blocks made by the Pratts themselves. The material of construction is all-important in the presentation of a closed façade on the public side, with windows well above eye level, while on the family side of the house there are floor-to-ceiling windows leading to the terrace and landscaping beyond.

# CHARLES T. WELTZHEIMER HOUSE

**Constructed:** 1948
**Address:** 127 Woodhaven Drive, Oberlin, Ohio 44074.

The Weltzheimer House is an "L" type residence constructed on a rectangular module of two by four feet. The original plan was constructed with the requests of the entire family as to what they required of a home from Wright in mind. Although this was common practice with the Usonian commissions, in this case the requests were for accommodation for the family dogs as well as for the more standard books and a piano.

The building materials are brick and redwood panels on plywood, with distinctive treatment of the mortar joints. However the major distinguishing feature of the Weltzheimer House is the treatment of the wooden cutouts of the clerestory windows beneath the redwood ceiling. These take the form of repeated circular motifs, apparently evoking the forms of the apple orchard on the site. Circular forms also decorate the roof molding. These decorative devices are unique in Usonian design, demonstrating the close collaboration between clients and architect.

RIGHT: Living room and terrace seen from the garden front. The terrace is protected by the broad overhang of the roof which is pierced to allow maximum sunlight to penetrate. The decorative motifs employed throughout the Weltzheimer House are unique, organic in form, and perhaps deriving their design from the apple orchard on the site of the house.

# ANNE AND ERIC V. BROWN HOUSE

**Constructed:** 1949
**Address:** 2806 Taliesin Drive, Kalamazoo, Michigan 49008.

For several of the original group, including Anne and Eric Brown who had formed the Acres in Galesburg, the original site for the projected homes was too distant from their working environment. The site of Parkwyn Village is nearer Kalamazoo and the original plan included several houses, although only four were built. The plan of the Brown House is constructed on a four foot unit module and it is designed as an in-line Usonian with views from the living room and terrace across to Lorenz Lake. The large workspace at the back of the living room leads on to a tunnel gallery with the four bedrooms, which include a dormitory-style children's bedroom, and the bathrooms together with a maid's bedroom leading off it. The roof of the structure is gabled, and like the other Parkwyn Village houses, the materials of construction are concrete textile block with mahogany trim.

LEFT: View of entrance façade. The roof line of the Brown House is at ground level, with gables for added height and interest. The concrete textile blocks of the construction are pierced on the street side to give a sense of privacy onto Taliesin Drive, while the living room has large windows and a view towards Lorenz Lake.

# HELEN AND WARD MCCARTNEY HOUSE

**Constructed:** 1949
**Address:** 2662 Taliesin Drive, Kalamazoo, Michigan 49008.

The McCartney House is one of four Usonian houses built in Parkwyn Village on a site southwest of Kalamazoo and designed by Wright in response to a group of young professionals who admired his work and ideals and wished to build their homes themselves. McCartney and Eric Brown, owner of a neighboring house, acted as their own contractors in cooperating on the making of the textile blocks for their houses.

The McCartney House is built on an additive principle, beginning as a core of a living and dining room with workspace in the form of an equilateral parallelogram, the bedroom wing was added four months later. The carport was added later still and the entrance was also enclosed. Like the house itself they were constructed from textile block with mahogany trim. In true Wrightian manner, the Parkwyn Village houses were integrated with their site by the planting of nearly 2,000 trees, although the entire village concept was never realized.

ABOVE: Exterior view of living room façade. The Parkwyn Village houses offered maximum privacy on their garden side and were subtly integrated into the wooded landscaped setting which is near Lorenz Lake to the southwest of Kalamazoo, within commuting distance of the clients' work.

# ROBERT AND GLORIA BERGER HOUSE

**Constructed:** 1950
**Address:** 259 Redwood Road, San Anselmo, California 94960.

Robert and Gloria Berger built their own house, a true Usonian design at a very basic level, as the Bergers were working with a very restricted budget of only $15,000. They had expert guidance through the project, which was specially adapted to do-it-yourself construction, from Aaron Green who had studied at Taliesin and became a close friend of Wright's. Green was associated with him on several projects in California, including the Rosenbaum House. The house is in the form of an equilateral parallelogram, with a hexagonal living room, and as in the McCartney House, the original master bedroom and bathroom were positioned on either side of the workspace. Two other bedrooms and a workshop complete an in-line plan.

The building stone is Sonoma, or Santa Rosa candy rock, and was split by Bob Berger, who blocked and tackled the stone and concrete of the construction himself.

LEFT: Entrance façade. One of the Usonian principles was that, given the economic standard plan and layout together with consultation and advice, it should be possible for clients to economize on materials and labor by doing some of the work themselves. Robert and Gloria Berger, who were on a strictly limited budget, put this idea into practice in their unique house.

RIGHT: Interior of living room, looking toward the hearth. The living room is hexagonal with the grid of its construction incised into the concrete floor. The Bergers did much of the work themselves, splitting the stone used for cladding and fixing it into the concrete construction. The locally occurring stone is Santa Rosa candy rock or Sonoma, used to dramatic effect both internally and externally.

# WILBUR C. PEARCE HOUSE

**Constructed:** 1950
**Address:** 5 Bradbury Hills Road, Bradbury, California 91010.

The Pearce House is distinguished by its site, on a steep ridge on a foothill of the San Gabriel Mountains in the Bradbury Hills. The orientation enables it to command views from its living room south to the San Gabriel valley and Los Angeles beyond, while to the north there are fine views of the mountains and the Mount Wilson Observatory. The living room opens onto an elliptical lily pond, flower border, and broad curved terrace. The steep site also requires that the roof and carport have steel cantilevering. The house is constructed on a three foot square unit module made from standard concrete block. The most extensive wooden areas, such as the ceilings and rafters, are made from Douglas fir, while Honduras mahogany, an especially warm-toned wood, is used to give contrast of color and texture to the prevailing neutrality of the concrete both internally and externally.

RIGHT: View of the house from the northeast. Constructed from concrete block using a three foot square unit module, the house commands a spectacular site in the foothills of the San Gabriel Mountains. Its site determines its structure: the cantilevered carport has to be anchored with steel bolts through its concrete floor, while the dramatic roof of the entire structure is also cantilevered with steel.

# ROBERT D. WINN HOUSE

**Constructed:** 1950
**Address:** 2822 Taliesin Drive, Kalamazoo, Michigan 49008.

The Winn House is unique among the Parkwyn Village houses. Robert Winn came late to the Village and selected a Usonian–based design that resembles the house built by Wright in 1949 for Kenneth and Phyllis Laurent in Rockford, Illinois, which is a single-story solar hemicycle, designed as a continuous flow of space for Mr Laurent to negotiate in his wheelchair. The Winn House is set on a hillside with a half basement which contains a guest bedroom, laundry, and utilities. The hillside created problems, not least in that the usual concrete pad and gravity heating had to be abandoned and forced air heating used instead. The site necessitated the use of cantilevering to support the porch and pierced roof. The wide curved porch with its roof pierced with skylights is protected by a screen, the length of the living and dining areas.

ABOVE: Exterior view. The curved porch of the Winn House is its most distinctive feature. Cantilevered above a half basement because the hillside site presented problems of construction, the roof of the porch is pierced with square skylights, and the space itself is screened so that it can be used as an outdoor extension of the living space.

# ROLAND AND RONNY REISLEY HOUSE

**Constructed:** 1951
**Address:** 44 Usonia Road, Pleasantville, New York 10570.

Usonia Homes, or Usonia II, as it is sometimes known, began building in 1947 on a 97 acre site within commuting distance of New York City as a result of the initiative of a group of friends. It was to be Wright's largest community, although the community center was never built while Wright and his apprentices were to design only 24 of the 48 houses. The Reisley House is the last Wright was to design for the project and is in many ways the most complex and exciting. The house is built on a triangular module, to which an addition was made in 1956, effectively doubling the space, and adding a separate dining room, children's bedrooms, a

bathroom, and a playroom. Like other Pleasantville Homes, the Reisley House is constructed from granite quarried from a nearby site and cypress. The rough-hewn masonry serves to further integrate the house into its wooded site.

ABOVE: Exterior view of west side balcony and lower level. The Reisley House was the last of the 24 houses to be designed by Wright for Usonia Homes, or Usonia II as it was known, in what had been planned as a unique community within commuting distance of New York City. The house uses rough-hewn local stone and cypress wood paneling throughout—even the shower has cypress paneling.

# KARL KUNDERT MEDICAL CLINIC

**Constructed:** 1955
**Address:** 1106 Pacific Street, San Luis Obispo, California 93401.

The Karl Kundert Medical Clinic represents an ingenious application of Usonian principles to the functions of a clinic of Opthalmology. Essentially it is a standard "L" Usonian house plan, adapted to the needs of patients needing treatment for eye diseases. It was originally planned to be built of textile block but was eventually built in brick with a perforated wooden clerestory and large windows in the reception space. The truncated "L" shape has at its center a large reception and waiting room distinguished by three tiers of clerestory windows of a distinctive cut-out design and filled with translucent glass. This spacious, high ceilinged lighted space is in marked contrast to the examination and treatment rooms which are windowless.

ABOVE: Reception area with triple-level clerestory showing the waiting area. An ingenious adaptation of the living room space in a Usonian house, the reception area is high ceilinged with three rows of perforated wooden panels in a unique design, forming a clerestory filled with translucent glass. The light is thus subtly filtered from above while eye-level windows filled with clear glass provide daylight.

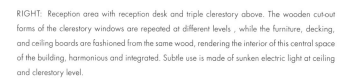

RIGHT: Reception area with reception desk and triple clerestory above. The wooden cut-out forms of the clerestory windows are repeated at different levels , while the furniture, decking, and ceiling boards are fashioned from the same wood, rendering the interior of this central space of the building, harmonious and integrated. Subtle use is made of sunken electric light at ceiling and clerestory level.

# CARL POST HOUSE (BORAH POST HOUSE)

**Constructed:** 1957
**Address:** 265 Donlea Road, Barrington Hills, Illinois 60010.

The Post House is an Erdman prefab unit designed by Wright in conjunction with the Marshall Erdman Company of Madison, Wisconsin. Two designs were produced, the Post House is based on Prefab Number One, constructed in Maidson in October 1956. The idea of the kit of prefabricated parts was to extend the model homes as low-cost housing to those who needed them most. However the cost of the prefabricated kits put them beyond the reach of most people, making them ideal for those who could not afford a custom-built Wright house from, as Wright himself put it, "Upper middle income groups, (but) not for low-cost housing." The grid for the Post House was a standard four foot unit which allowed for a four bedroom space with a living and dining room space as well as spaces designated for use as "kitchen" and "family" on

the plan, rather than the workspace of the custom-built Usonian. Builder Al Borah sold the house to Carl Post in the year of its construction in 1957.

ABOVE: View of house from grounds. The Post House is one of a series of Erdman prefabs, which offered different configurations of a basic kit of prefabricated parts. The Post House is a four-bedroom model with a large master bedroom and an exposed basement. It also has a garage rather than the more usual carport.

# CARL SCHULTZ HOUSE

**Constructed:** 1957
**Address:** 2704 Highland Ct, St Joseph, Michigan 49085.

The Schultz House occupies a dramatic site on the left bank of the Saint Joseph River, commanding fine views from its living room terrace which is supported by cantilevering over a ravine. The unit module for the in-line configuration is a four foot square. The house, while built to Usonian principles, is designed on a large scale, measuring some 3,850 square feet. The bedroom wing has a 56 foot tunnel gallery from which opens a large dormitory-style bedroom in addition to two other bedrooms and bathrooms and a utilities basement together with a lower basement. The "quiet wing" is completed by an elaborate games room measuring some 16 by 20 feet, an unusual feature in a Usonian house, even for one on such a large scale as this. There is also a library and guest bedroom situated with the master bedroom off the living area, which has a separate dining area.

LEFT: Exterior view of living room terrace. The exceptionally wide terrace of the Schultz House is cantilevered over a ravine on the left bank of the St Joseph River, commanding fine views at tree-top height. The broad overhang of the roof is widely pierced to form a trellis, allowing maximum light through the floor-to-ceiling glass of the living room.

# DR. ROBERT G. AND MARY WALTON HOUSE

**Constructed:** 1957
**Address:** 147 Hogue Road, Modesto, California 95350.

This exceptionally large house was built on a 32 inch unit (of two concrete textile blocks) and is a development of the ideas demonstrated in the New York Usonian Exhibition house concept of 1953. This fully realized in-line Usonian was built on the site of what was to be the Solomon Guggenheim Museum in New York City, which began building three years later. The house received maximum publicity and was auctioned and moved when building on the Guggenheim began. The Walton House was but one development of the exhibition house, one that solved the problem of housing a very large family by placing four bedrooms in line off a long gallery and completing the "L" with a playroom, thus effectively creating a children's wing, with the master bedroom and another bedroom or study on the other side of the gallery. The Modesto climate necessitated the provision of air conditioning and perimeter heat, and the house retains much of its original furniture designed by Wright.

RIGHT: Exterior view of private façade. The Walton House is exceptionally large and at nearly 3,000 square feet, it is one of the largest single-story homes to be designed by Wright. The family façade has views out on to the lake and beyond while the public façade ensures maximum privacy with a double range of small clerestory windows set high into the concrete.

# INDEX